EAR TRAINING

**A Comprehensive Approach to the Systematic
Study of Melodic and Harmonic Structures in Music**

VOLUME I

SCALE FORMS
through
SIX BASIC TETRACHORDS

Elvo S. D'Amante
Former Chairman: Department of Music
Laney Community College
Oakland, California

Address orders and editorial correspondence to:
Encore Music Publishing Co.
P.O. Box 315
Orinda, CA 94563-2702

ISBN: 0-9620941-2-9

Printed in the United States of America

10 9 8 7 6 5 4 3 2 1

To my grandchildren

Table of Contents

Chapter I
Materials for Study

Chapter II
Guidelines for Study

Chapter III
Singing Drills & CD Lessons

Chapter IV
CD Answers

Chapter IV (Continued)
CD Answers

Preface

To the student:

Ear Training in three volumes is a comprehensive approach for the systematic study of melodic and harmonic structures used by musicians during the past four hundred years. These resource guides are designed to teach, improve, strengthen, and enhance one's understanding of the basic tools that make up the sounds of music. The need for an accurate, aural understanding of simple and complex melodic and harmonic invention is a must for every performing musician. Each student of music, amateur or professional, or, for that matter, anyone pursuing an avocational or recreational need will certainly benefit by the materials and aural skill studies provided in these three volumes.

Each volume contains parallel chapters entitled, *Materials for Study*, *Guidelines for Study*, *Study Drills*, and **CD Answers**. The contents of these chapters change with the specific intent of each volume. Volume I is entitled, *Scale Forms through Six Basic Tetrachords*; Volume II, *Twelve Basic Interval Sounds to Master*; and Volume III, *Capturing the Basic Chord Qualities*. Answers to the compact disc lessons are to be found in the final chapter of each volume. It is recommended that you read and understand the chapters entitled, *Materials for Study* and *Guidelines for Study* for the specific volume before attempting the drills and lessons pertaining to that particular volume. Although the preferred course of study of these three volumes should proceed in the order in which they are presented, taking chapter studies out of order in each volume or across volumes may be beneficial for those who have a more advanced background in music. For those students interested in enhancing their total understanding of these volumes of ear training, two additional books written by this author are readily available and are entitled, *Music Fundamentals* and *All About Chords*. These books provide the supportive background for the materials presented in each volume.

The development of one's ear represents one of the most significant steps towards excellence in music. Be patient. Treat the drills in this book as you would if you were embarking on a singing career or becoming a fine instrumentalist. The process of practice is the same. Developing your visual and aural memory is of paramount importance. Best of luck for continued success in music.

The author

Acknowledgments

Many musicians have shaped the contents of *Ear Training* in *Volumes I, II, & III*. They have contributed suggestions, time, and support for this grand project. I'm indebted to all of them and, specifically, to Dix Bruce, a former student, excellent musician, and, himself, a very prolific author of books on the many aspects of music performance. His help, in the making of CDs for these Volumes was indispensable; I'm grateful for his expertise. To Jim Lynch, a former student and excellent musician, I owe a vote of thanks for his patience, effort, and devotion to this project. He has certainly been endowed with an eagle eye and a marvelous ear. He helped in many ways by making excellent editing suggestions. His efforts were invaluable and extremely appreciated. For her knowledge of computer graphics and her artistic touch, I'm indebted to Charlotte Gibb, another musician. Each volume cover is extremely tasteful and creative. Her contributions as well as each of the other above named contributors were always forthcoming, valuable and, again, extremely appreciated.

I would be remiss if I didn't acknowledge the enormous debt of gratitude that I feel for those who helped pave the way for my pursuit of excellence in the teaching of music theory and performance, especially students who challenged my very musical existence daily in the classroom; for all their efforts, I'm extremely grateful.

I shall never forget the knowledge given to me during my formative years as a young aspiring musician by two of the world's finest composer/teachers: Darius Milhaud and Roger Sessions. They demonstrated truly remarkable patience and expert guidance in my pursuit of musical excellence. I shall always be mindful and thankful for their direction and, above all, their inspiration.

SCALE FORMS
through
SIX BASIC TETRACHORDS

CHAPTER

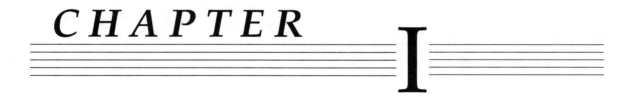

I

Materials for Study

Materials for Study

Six Basic Tetrachords

Six basic tetrachords, in various combinations, form the basis for traditional scales of the past four hundred years. They function as a reservoir of sound for modal scales, chromatic scales, major scales, minor scales (three forms), pentatonic scales, and whole-tone scales. A tetrachord is a series of four notes that forms a specific intervallic structure when played successively in a scalelike form; moreover, when playing a tetrachord in its ascending or descending form, its sound always remains the same. Understanding this very significant detail of tetrachord construction is extremely important.

Tetrachords represent the first stage of study in the training of one's ear. Additionally, they are invaluable to the study of music theory and performance. They form the basis for the material to be presented in this book.

Example 1

The six basic tetrachords.

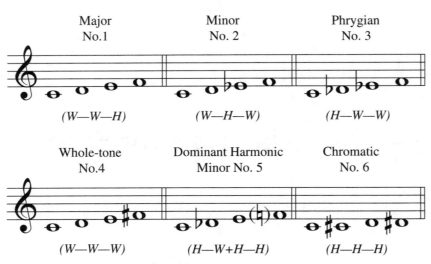

W = Whole Step; H = Half Step; W+H = Whole Step plus a half step.

The Seven Modes

The first four of the six basic tetrachords form the basis for all modal scales. Using these tetrachords in various combinations and in succession will formulate **the seven modes**: the *Ionian, Dorian, Phrygian, Lydian, Mixolydian, Aeolian,* and *Locrian.* The modes that begin with the letter "L" (*Lydian* and *Locrian*) use a half-step hookup between each successive tetrachord, while all others use a whole step. Again, as we have stated earlier, each tetrachord must sound the same whether ascending or descending. Therefore, when performing tetrachords No. 1 [W-W-H/**H-W-W**] and No. 3 [H-W-W/**W-W-H**] reverse them—as shown in bold print—to achieve the same intervallic sound descending as well as ascending. All other tetrachords present no problems because their intervallic relationships remain the same in either direction.

In Example 2 on pages 4 and 5, it is important to note that two modes—the *Ionian* and *Aeolian*—form the basis for diatonic major and minor scales. Also, it is important to know that no two modes share the same half-step pattern and that the order of modal presentation allows for an easy method for memorizing their construction. Table 1 is presented as a reference and a visual guide for memorizing the order and sequential relationship of modes.

Finally, knowing that the Ionian uses two No. 1 tetrachords, the Dorian uses two No. 2 tetrachords, the Phrygian uses two No. 3 tetrachords, etc., is significant. In addition, knowing that the sequence of tetrachord numbers represents a specific order is also significant. The memorization of modal order is helped by using association and imagination as basic memory ingredients. The following (ungrammatical) sentence will help in the process.

If (**I**onian) **D**ori (**D**orian) **p**lays (**P**hrygian)
like (**L**ydian) **me** (**M**ixolydian), **all's** (**A**eolian) **l**ost (**L**ocrian).

Table 1	■	Modal Synthesis
Modal Names		**Tetrachord Order**
Ionian		No. **1** followed by No. 1
Dorian		No. **2** followed by No. 2
Phrygian		No. **3** followed by No. 3
● Lydian		No. **4** followed by No. 1
Mixolydian		No. **1** followed by No. 2
Aeolian		No. **2** followed by No. 3
● Locrian		No. **3** followed by No. 4

● Half-step hookups for the Lydian and the Locrian; all others use the whole step.

Example 2

The tetrachord structures involving the seven modes.

(1) The Ionian

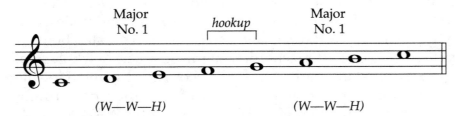

(2) The Dorian

(3) The Phrygian

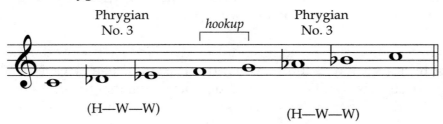

(4) The Lydian

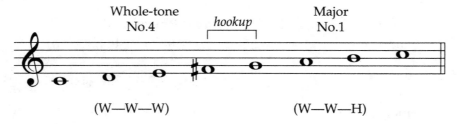

(5) The Mixolydian

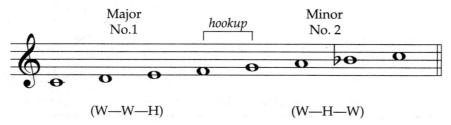

(6) The Aeolian

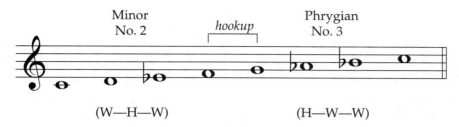

(7) The Locrian

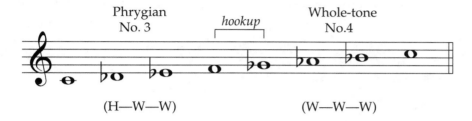

The Chromatic Scale

The ascending form of the **chromatic scale** (12-tone) contains three consecutively placed No. 6 (chromatic) tetrachords. The recommended procedure for writing chromatic scales involves the use of sharps ascending and flats descending. Although other methods of writing chromatic scales are equally correct, performing musicians prefer sharps ascending and flats descending. The hookup between tetrachords is one-half step. When writing the descending form of the chromatic scale, start with the upper keynote and use three consecutively placed No. 6 (chromatic) tetrachords descending, using flats instead of sharps.

Example 3
The tetrachord structure involving the chromatic scale.

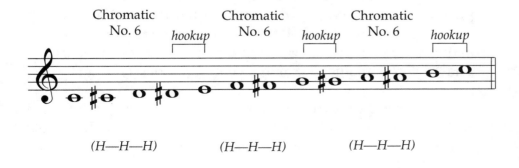

The Major Scale

The **major scale** contains two successive No.1 (major) tetrachords and sounds the same whether ascending or descending. Remember to reverse the No. 1 (major) tetrachord when writing the descending form of the scale. The first tetrachord starts on the keynote (the tonic degree) of the scale. The second tetrachord starts on the fifth degree of the scale that is the *dominant* scale degree. The *hookup* interval between the two successive tetrachords is the distance of one whole step. Together these tetrachords, when placed consecutively and separated by a whole step hookup, serve as the basis for all major scales.

The major scale structure is as follows:

Example 4
The tetrachord structures involving the major scale.

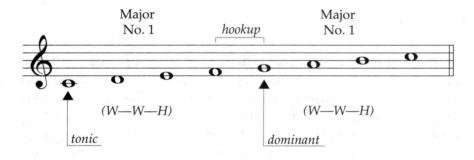

The Minor Scale

There are three forms of the **minor scale**: the *Aeolian*, the *harmonic*, and the *melodic*. While each scale form is unique, they share the same tonic minor tetrachord. The dominant tetrachord contains the primary difference between these scale forms.

The **Aeolian form** (sometimes referred to as the **natural** or **pure** minor) contains a No. 2 (minor) tetrachord placed on its tonic degree and a No. 3 (Phrygian) on its dominant degree. As in the major scale, the hookup remains the same—one whole step. The Aeolian remains the same ascending or descending.

The **harmonic form** contains, a No. 2 (minor) tetrachord and a No. 5 (dominant harmonic minor) tetrachord with a whole step hookup. The harmonic form ascends and descends in the same manner.

As with the Aeolian and harmonic minor forms, the No. 2 (minor) tetrachord serves as the tonic tetrachord in the **melodic form.** Ascending and descending forms, however, are different; the ascending form contains a No. 1 (major) tetrachord placed on its dominant degree while the descending form is the Aeolian minor scale–a No. 3 (Phrygian) tetrachord followed by a No. 2 (Minor) tetrachord. The hookup in the ascending and descending forms is the same as in all minor scale forms–one whole step. Pay particular attention to the reverse structure of the descending No. 3 (Phrygian) tetrachord; this reversed structure ensures the same sound as the ascending counterpart.

Study carefully the ascending and descending scale forms of the minor scale. It is imperative that one understand the construction of these unique scale forms before attempting the study of ear training.

Example 5
The tetrachord structures involving the three forms of the minor: the Aeolian, the harmonic, and the melodic.

(1) Aeolian form

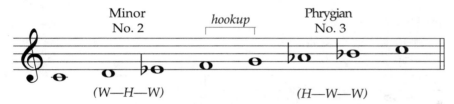

(2) Harmonic form

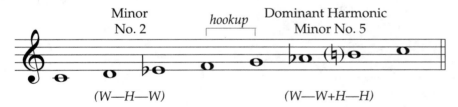

(3) Melodic form, ascending and descending

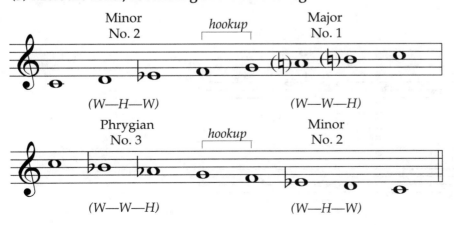

The Pentatonic Scale

The **Pentatonic scale** contains five notes and uses two abbreviated tetrachords. Two forms exist for this study: the major pentatonic based upon its parallel major scale and the minor pentatonic based upon its parallel Aeolian form of the minor scale. When removing the *fourth* (4) and *seventh* (7) degrees of a major scale, a major pentatonic scale forms. In a very similar manner, a minor pentatonic scale forms when removing the *second* (2) and *sixth* (6) degrees of an Aeolian minor scale.

Pay particular attention in the example to the major and minor relationships involving their respective tetrachords and the selected scale degrees that are removed when forming both pentatonic scales. Both major and minor pentatonic scales are presented immediately below their parallel major and minor (Aeolian) scales.

Example 6

The tetrachord structures involving both pentatonic scales.

(1) Major

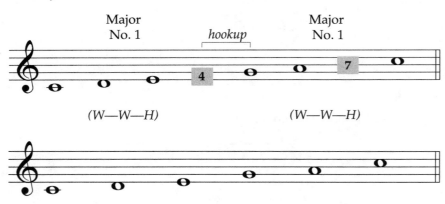

(2) Minor

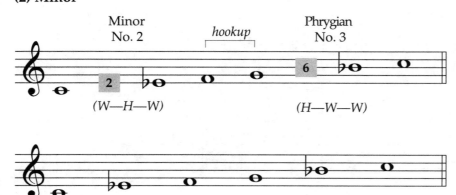

The Whole-tone Scale

The **Whole-tone Scale**, as the name implies, contains **six whole steps** and uses two overlapping tetrachords. The fourth degree of the first tetrachord becomes the first degree of the second tetrachord. Although this appears to be a confusing notion, it is a rather simple idea that serves as an ideal way to learn the singing, playing, and hearing of this aurally–complex scale. For many musicians, this scale is one of the most difficult to learn. Because of the overlapping of tetrachords, there is no concern for the all–important hookup that was previously presented in other scale forms.

Example 7
The tetrachord structures involving the whole-tone scale.

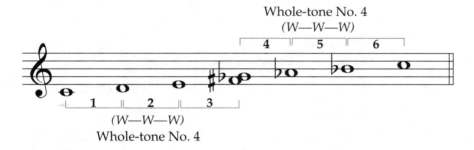

MANUSCRIPT PRACTICE
Use empty staves for note taking and drill.

SCALE FORMS
through
SIX BASIC TETRACHORDS

CHAPTER  **II**

Guidelines for Study

Guidelines for Study

The presentation of tetrachord usage as it involves scale construction plays a very important role in the study of ear training. Scales in their various tetrachord patterns serve as the reservoir of sounds for melodic and harmonic invention. On a daily basis, one hears music compositions that use major and/or minor tonal centers coupled with modal invention, chromatic, pentatonic, and whole–tone influences. Classically–oriented musicians, jazz, rock, and commercial musicians all use tetrachords in one way or other, abbreviated or otherwise. Tetrachords are the key ingredient found in all the avenues of musical invention, including improvisation and composition; they create the basis and foundation for this study of ear training.

The Piano

If you are an instrumentalist, it is imperative that you sing and play on your instrument and/or the **piano** each given tetrachord and scale. Occasionally, when singing these exercises, some of the material will go beyond your vocal range. If this occurs, adjust the part to make it comfortable for performance. It's important to *make* the pitches and, of course, to play and sing them in tune. If your instrument is voice, sing as well as play each tetrachord or scale on the piano. Of course, the piano should be in tune for obvious reasons.

Use the piano in the following manner:

1. to give a starting pitch when singing an exercise,

2. to demonstrate the intervallic sounds of a particular tetrachord or exercise,

3. to validate what has been sung, and

4. to help develop a discriminating ear for discerning the differences that occur between component parts of a musical expression.

When using the piano to obtain a starting pitch, sound the keynote before you begin singing. Make sure that you have firmly chosen the correct pitch and then continue with the exercise. Generally, playing along with the exercise as you sing will do very little in the way of training your ear; however, if you are having difficulty in *making* the pitches, it is wise to play along with the vocal rendition. This will help to eliminate the problem of pitch insecurity and provide the necessary solution to improving pitch and intonation through matching. After sensing a better understanding of the material, however, discontinue the matching approach.

Occasionally, it is important to check various segments of each exercise. This accomplishes two things: it provides an opportunity to monitor each endeavor and helps to strengthen good intonation. Playing the material back and hearing it for immediate reinforcement is a valuable aid in the development of one's ear.

Transposition

Occasionally, it may be necessary to use **transposition** (the moving of tetrachord patterns or musical segments to other keynotes) to perform some of the exercises. For singers this should not cause any real problems with the exception of range; however, for instrumentalists the moving and subsequent performance of tetrachord patterns or musical segments may involve clef changes, range considerations, and difficult fingering combinations. Make every effort to allow for a comfortable solution to the problem. The raising or lowering of an octave for a particular portion of a tetrachord, scale, or exercise is perfectly all right; improving and enhancing the performance of an exercise in this manner is beneficial. Feel free to use whatever musical means necessary to accomplish the act of singing, playing, and hearing the musical excerpt presented. In the following example, pay particular attention to the technique of transposing a tetrachord to various keynotes and the use of the reverse form of the descending No. 1 (major) tetrachord.

Example 8
An example of transposed tetrachords with the ascending as well as the reversed descending forms.

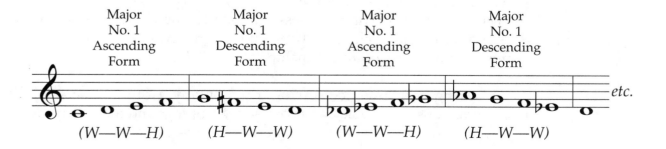

Regular, Broken and Abbreviated Tetrachords

Using **regular** tetrachord forms represents the first step in training your ear; however, there are other forms that are equally productive for study, and in one form or another provide additional musical results. **Broken** tetrachords are those that do not use scale forms but tend to skip around. **Abbreviated** tetrachords are those that have missing notes as in the pentatonic major and minor scales. There are definite advantages for studying these different tetrachord forms; they provide an expanded potential for learning in the study of intervals.

Example 9
Examples of broken and abbreviated tetrachords.

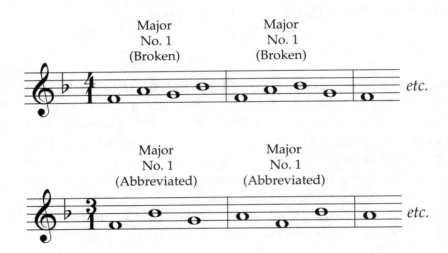

Rhythmic Groupings

The superimposition of various **rhythmic groupings** on tetrachords and/or scales is a good idea. It places the brain in a more active mode and eliminates the non-thinking processes that often occur in drill studies. It provides for more critical, instant decision making in the process of combining pitch with rhythm. Practice sessions that are fresh and interesting are more enjoyable and rewarding. An additional reason for using these rhythmic groupings is to provide for a creative avenue during the practice session. Finally, the ability to include rhythmic invention along with melodic invention helps to establish a more secure sense of musicianship.

During each practice session, do as many groupings and/or combinations as possible. Start with easy groupings and then progress to a more difficult level as the materials become more secure in your mind. The following examples provide rhythmic groupings as well as different combinations for use with superimposition. Study each rhythmic grouping very carefully.

Example 10(a)
Recommended rhythmic groupings for the superimpostion of tetrachords and scales.

Quarter Note, Eighth Note, Triplet, and Sixteenth Note Groupings.

Example 10(b)
More advanced and recommended rhythmic groupings for the superimpostion of tetrachords and scales.

Combined Rhythmic Groupings.

Example 10(c)

The superimpostion of two rhythmic groupings on tetrachords.

A combined rhythmic grouping [Ex. 10(b) #3] using a No. 1 (major) tetrachord.

A combined rhythmic grouping [Ex. 10(b) #1] using a No. 2 (minor) tetrachord.

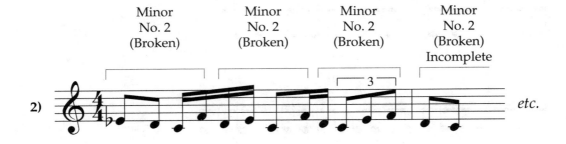

The Mixing of Materials.

The **mixing of materials** for the purposes of improving and training your ear is a valuable avenue of study. It is not part of the beginner's regime, but, rather, a method for those who have established a more thorough understanding of the materials. For example, after several sessions of study involving individual tetrachords, sing and play a mixture of them. The introduction of limited new material into an established mode of practice can be very productive. A good axiom to follow with new material is as follows: if the material feels comfortable the first time through, make it part of your standard repertoire of practice. With the necessary repetitive drills to follow, the new materials will become part of your standard program of practice very quickly and provide a greater feeling of accomplishment, progress, and gratification.

Example 11
The mixing of materials.

(1) A mixture of tetrachords.

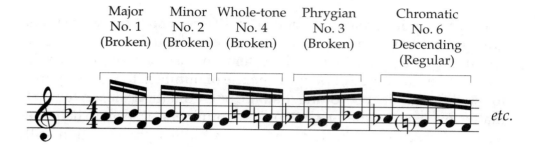

(2) An ascending and descending form of two different modal scales.

Dictation

Two compact discs are included with Volume One. They concern materials discussed in Chapters I and II, namely the six basic tetrachords with their broken and arpeggiated versions. In addition the combining of these six basic tetrachords into scale forms is also presented. The goal of these drills is to strengthen your ear and provide the ability to quickly identify various scale forms. The sense of capturing in one's ear the sound of these combined tetrachords and their variations will pave the way to musical excellence and success.

Using the CD involves the practice of taking what is referred to as dictation, a method whereby the student is asked to reproduce on paper what has been previously played. Each exercise is short and concise. In most studies presented, a short pitch (middle c) is sustained before each exercise to help orient the listener's ear. It is meant solely to provide a means for identifying the starting note of the ensuing tetrachord . In later studies, the use of a security pitch (such as middle c) will not be necessary and will not be given. In most instances, individual measures of each exercise will be played twice. After each exercise is given, a short pause will be provided on the CD to allow sufficient time (make every effort to work within the allotted time limits) to reproduce the desirable response.

Different Methods or Systems are Applicable for Singing

In the pursuit of developing a good ear, **different methods or systems are applicable for the singing** of exercises. The use of a diatonic or chromatic solfeggio (do, re, mi) system; the use of a single syllable (la) for an entire range of pitches; the use of numbers that correspond to the different degrees of the diatonic or chromatic scale; or, for that matter, even city names used in place of numbers all seem to help the learning process. With all of these possibilities, the question still persists as to which method or system is best? For those familiar with the chromatic system of solfeggio, it is, perhaps, the more effective method of study; however, the use of the single syllable (la) system seems to work, effectively; it is especially helpful and less stressful when having to sing chromatic or atonal passages.

University and college music instructors are not unanimous in their preference for a particular method or system; however, they are unanimous about the importance of singing particular exercises for the improvement of the ear. On this point, there is no debate. Therefore, it is imperative that each exercise be sung as often as is necessary to achieve the necessary degree of understanding. With the familiarity and understanding of the recommended materials, excellent results will take place and the pace of learning will be quick.

Choose the system that works well for you and stick with it. As was previously stated, the single syllable (la) system is, perhaps, the simplest system to use. Remember that the purpose of singing is not to develop a great voice but, rather, to develop a great ear. The ability to reproduce what has been heard, sung, or played is a very valuable and incalculable asset to the musician.

Manuscript Practice
Use empty staves for note taking and drill.

Scale Forms

through

Six Basic Tetrachords

CHAPTER

III

Singing Drills & CD Lessons

Singing Drill #1

Instructions: Singing Drill #1 is a twenty–four measure study of the regular No. 1 (major) tetrachord in all of its possible versions. When performing this study, attempt to gain a sense of each intervallic relationship. Sing it several times in a slow and thoughtful manner, increasing your speed as you gain a more thorough understanding of the materials. Remember to use the piano wisely; use it to secure your first pitch and then, from time to time, check your correctness of pitch and your intonation. You may even add rhythmic interest to heighten the learning process. Your goal is to stay on pitch and do the entire drill without faltering.

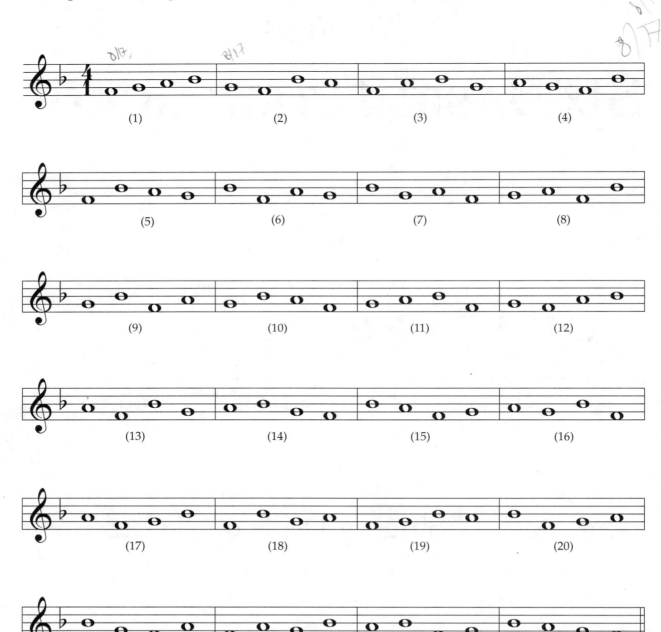

CD Lesson #1

CD #1 Tracks #2 (3:11) & #3 (3:09)

Instructions: CD Lesson #1 presents two studies of the regular and broken forms of the No. 1 (major) tetrachord. Treat these studies as dictation exercises and fill in the notation in the blank measures provided below. Listen carefully and rely on your memory before writing. It is impossible to write as quickly as someone else can play; therefore, work on improving your memory and concentrating on each measure before writing. If you are having difficulty, feel free to use the pause button on your CD machine. Each measure will be played twice. Before the first playing of each measure, a sounding pitch will be given reflecting the first note of each measure. No sounding pitch will be given for the repeated measure. Use the first (screened) measure of Study I as a model for the entire page. Answers to both studies are provided in the next chapter on page 56.

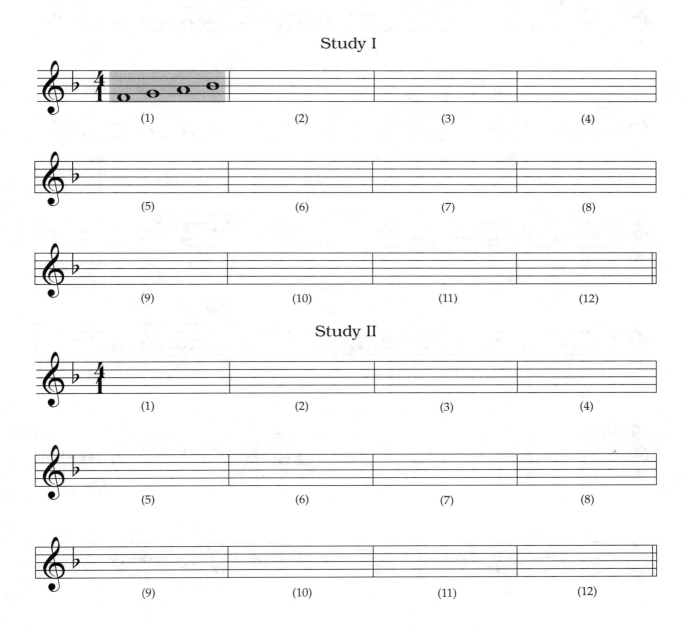

Study I

Study II

Singing Drill #2

Instructions: Singing Drill #2 is a twenty–four measure study of the regular No. 2 (minor) tetrachord in all of its possible versions. When performing this study, attempt to gain a sense of each intervallic relationship. Sing it several times in a slow and thoughtful manner, increasing your speed as you gain a more thorough understanding of the materials. Check for correctness of pitch and your intonation, from time to time, with the piano. Adding rhythmic interest can be extremely beneficial. Remember that your goal is to stay on pitch and to do the entire exercise without faltering.

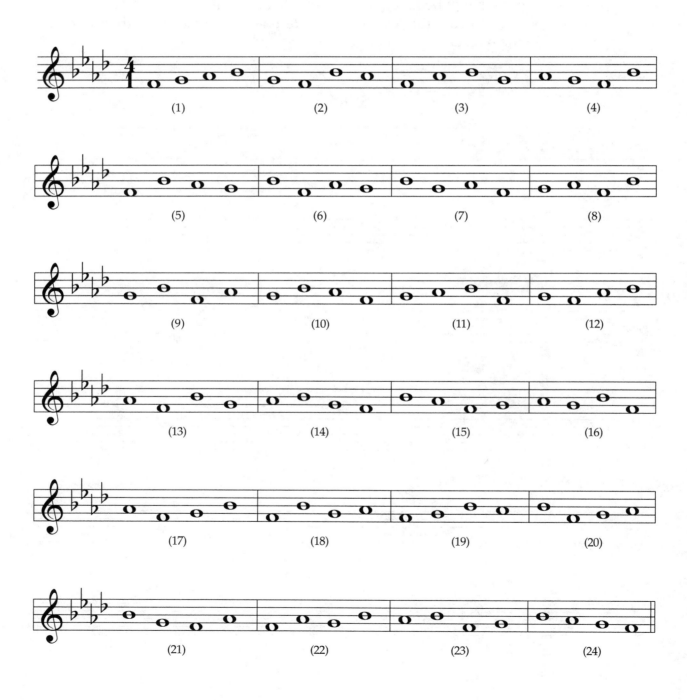

CD Lesson #2

Instructions: CD Lesson #2 presents two studies of the regular and broken forms of the No. 2 (minor) tetrachord. Treat these studies as dictation exercises and fill in the notation in the blank measures provided below. Listen carefully and rely on your memory before writing. If you are having difficulty, feel free to use the pause button on your CD machine; however, every effort should be made to stay within the time limits given on the CD. Each measure will be played twice. Before the first playing of each measure, a sounding pitch will be given reflecting the first note of each measure. No sounding pitch will be given for the repeated measure. It might be helpful to read the instruction given for CD Drill Study #1 (see page 27). Use the first (screened) measure of Study I as a model for the entire page. Answers to both studies are provided in the next chapter on page 56 & 57.

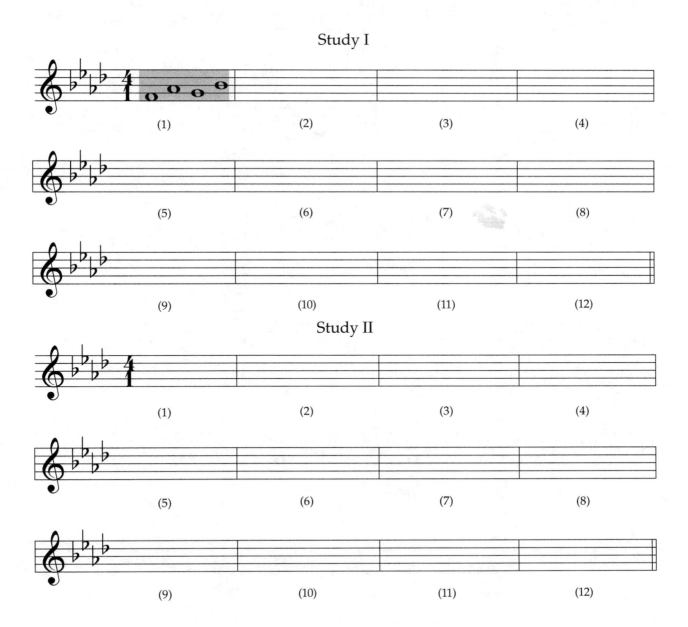

Singing Drill #3

Instructions: Singing Drill #3 is a twenty–four measure study of the regular No. 3 (Phrygian) tetrachord in all of its possible versions. Perform it as many times as is necessary to gain an understanding and familiarity of the materials. If you are having difficulty with one interval in particular, isolate it and study it out of context. After singing it several times, place it in context and see if it makes a difference. More than one attempt might be necessary to solve the problem. Follow the same instructions and comments given for Singing Drill #1 (see page 26).

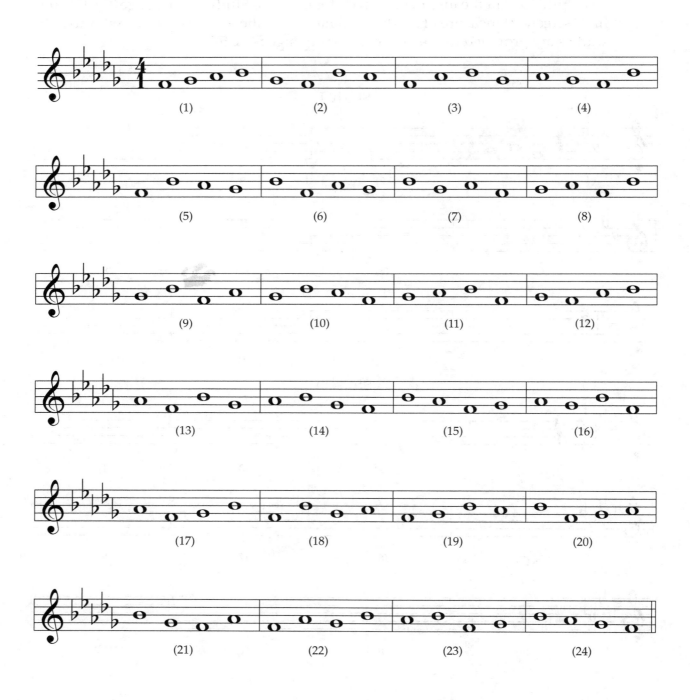

CD Lesson #3

Instructions: CD Lesson #3 presents two studies of the regular and broken forms of the No. 3 (Phrygian) tetrachord. Treat these studies as dictation exercises and fill in the notation in the blank measures provided below. Again, as in the previous dictation exercises, the method and routine remains the same. Each measure will be played twice. Before the first playing of each measure, a sounding pitch will be given reflecting the first note of each measure. No sounding pitch will be given for the repeated measure. Listen carefully to each measure and rely on your memory before writing. Use the first (screened) measure of Study I as a model for the entire page. Answers to both studies are given in the next chapter on page 57.

Singing Drill #4

Instructions: Singing Drill #4 is a twenty–four measure study of the regular No. 4 (whole–tone) tetrachord in all of its possible versions. The whole–tone tetrachord, often referred to as the Lydian tetrachord, contains an interval (f to b) referred to as a tritone. This interval, containing a span of three whole tones, is a very difficult interval to learn. Spend some time at the piano working on a better understanding of this complex interval; it won't be time wasted. After you have gained a greater familiarity with this interval, begin the study on this page. Also, the same instructions and comments given for Singing Drill #1 (see page 26) apply to this study.

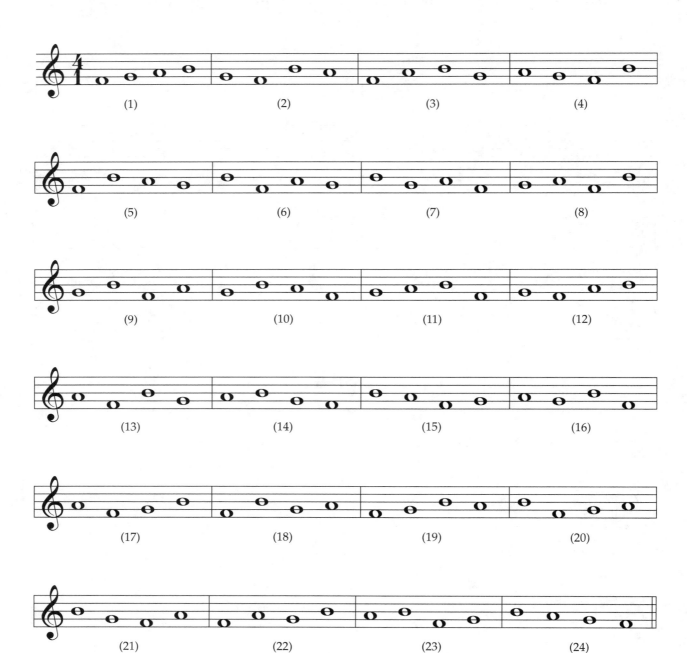

CD Lesson #4

CD#1 Tracks #8 (3:08) & #9 (3:24)

Instructions: CD Lesson #4 presents two studies of the regular and broken forms of the No. 4 (whole–tone) tetrachord. Treat these studies as dictation exercises and fill in the notation in the blank measures provided below. Again, as in the previous dictation exercises, the method and routine remains the same. Each measure will be played twice. Before the first playing of each measure, a sounding pitch will be given reflecting the first note of each measure. No sounding pitch will be given for the repeated measure. Listen carefully for the tritone in these studies; it occurs from time to time. Also, as with the previous drill studies, listen carefully and critically and remember to rely on your memory before writing. Use the first (screened) measure of Study I as a model for the entire page. Answers to both studies are given in the next chapter on page 58.

Study I

Study II

Singing Drill #5

Instructions: Singing Drill #5 is a twenty–four measure study of the regular No. 5 (dominant harmonic minor) tetrachord in all of its possible versions. This tetrachord contains between its second and third pitches (g♭ to a♮) another difficult interval to learn. This interval is an augmented second, and it is an important part of the harmonic minor scale. Spend some time at the piano with this interval before doing this study. After gaining a grasp of this complex interval, begin the study on this page. Also, the same instructions and comments apply to this study as were given for Singing Drill #1 (see page 26).

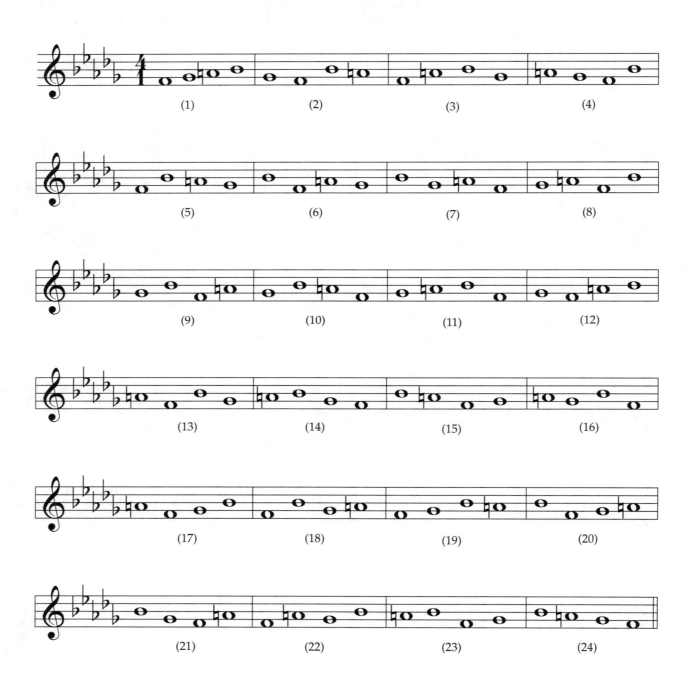

CD Lesson #5

Instructions: CD Lesson Study #5 contains two studies of the regular and broken forms of the No. 5 (dominant harmonic minor) tetrachord. Treat these drill studies as dictation exercises and fill in the notation in the blank measures provided below. Again, as in the previous dictation exercises, the method and routine remains the same. Each measure will be played twice. Before the first playing of each measure, a sounding pitch will be given reflecting the first note of each measure. No sounding pitch will be given for the repeated measure. The most difficult interval in this context (the augmented second) found in the No. 5 tetrachord occurs quite frequently in the following two studies. Be prepared for it. Use the first (screened) measure of Study I as a model for the entire page. Answers to both studies are provided in the next chapter on page 58 & 59.

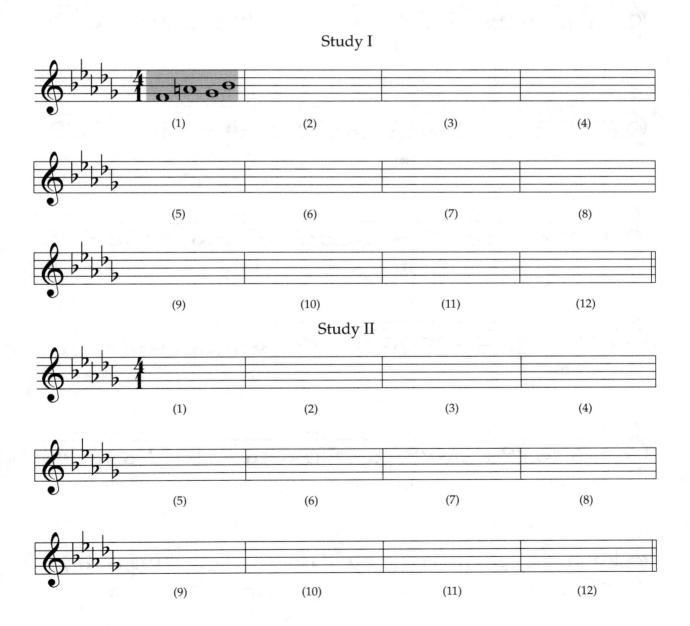

Study I

Study II

Singing Drill #6

Instructions: Singing Drill #6 is a twenty–four measure study of the regular No. 6 (chromatic) tetrachord in all of its possible versions. It is a very difficult singing study, but one that will pay huge dividends. Most importantly, it will not only help your ear but it will enhance your ability to read complex notation. The abundant mixture of flats and sharps helps provide the necessary drill that strengthens your reading ability. Also, the singing and viewing of complex intervals—for example, diminished thirds— is an additional benefit. Follow the same instructions and comments for this study as were given for Singing Drill #1 (see page 26).

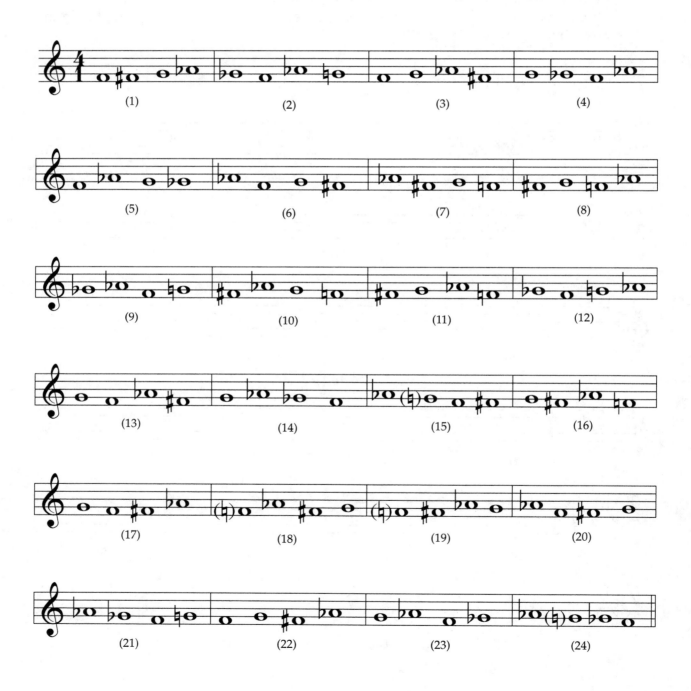

CD Lesson #6A   CD #1 Tracks #12 (3:28) & #13 (3:26)

Instructions: CD Lesson #6A contains two studies of the regular and broken forms of the No. 6 (chromatic) tetrachord. Treat these studies as dictation exercises and fill in the notation in the blank measures provided below. Again, as in the previous dictation exercises, the method and routine remains the same. Each measure will be played twice. A sounding pitch reflecting the first pitch of the measure will be played only once. No sounding pitch will be played on the repeat of the measure. Mixed chromatic and diatonic pitches can be very difficult to identify. Be patient. If you are having trouble, feel free to use the pause button on your CD machine; however, every effort should be made to work within the time limits given on the CD. Use the first (screened) measure of Study I as a model for the entire page. Answers to both studies are provided in the next chapter on page 59.

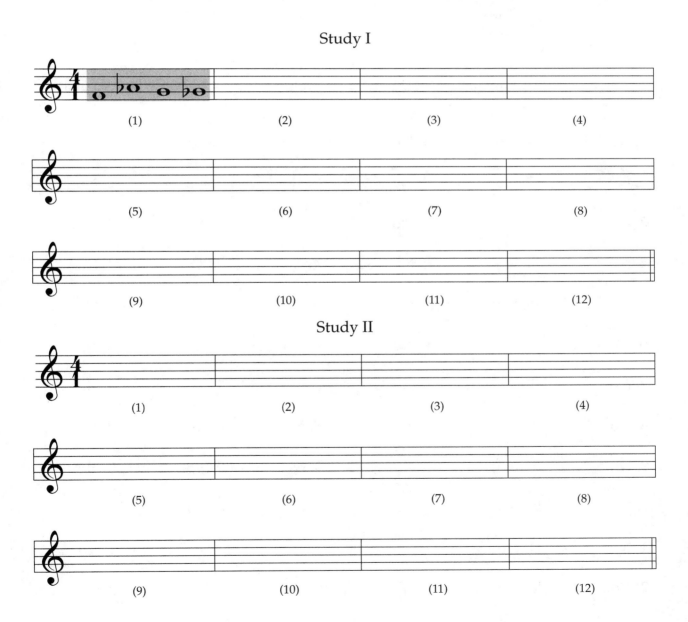

CD Lesson #6B

Instructions: CD Lesson #6B presents two studies. Study I contrasts the No. 1 (major) with the No. 2 (minor) tetrachords and Study II contrasts the No. 3 (Phrygian) with the No. 5 (dominant harmonic minor) tetrachords. Treat these studies as dictation exercises and fill in the blank spaces with the numbers of the corresponding and contrasting tetrachords in each column. Each ascending or descending tetrachord will be played twice with *no* sounding pitch. Listen carefully and rely on your memory before writing down your choice. Use the first (screened) answer of Study I as the model for the entire page. Answers to both studies are provided in the next chapter on page 60.

CD #1 Tracks #14(2:32) #15(2:22) #16(2:14)			CD #1 Tracks #17(2:19) #18(2:15) #19(2:10)		
Study I Contrasting No. 1 and No. 2			Study II Contrasting No. 3 and No. 5		
Column A	Column B	Column C	Column A	Column B	Column C
1. No. 1	1. No. ___	1. No. ___	1. No. ___	1. No. ___	1. No. ___
2. No. ___	2. No. ___	2. No. ___	2. No. ___	2. No. ___	2. No. ___
3. No. ___	3. No. ___	3. No. ___	3. No. ___	3. No. ___	3. No. ___
4. No. ___	4. No. ___	4. No. ___	4. No. ___	4. No. ___	4. No. ___
5. No. ___	5. No. ___	5. No. ___	5. No. ___	5. No. ___	5. No. ___
6. No. ___	6. No. ___	6. No. ___	6. No. ___	6. No. ___	6. No. ___
7. No. ___	7. No. ___	7. No. ___	7. No. ___	7. No. ___	7. No. ___
8. No. ___	8. No. ___	8. No. ___	8. No. ___	8. No. ___	8. No. ___
9. No. ___	9. No. ___	9. No. ___	9. No. ___	9. No. ___	9. No. ___
10. No. ___	10. No. ___	10. No. ___	10. No. ___	10. No. ___	10. No. ___
11. No. ___	11. No. ___	11. No. ___	11. No. ___	11. No. ___	11. No. ___
12. No. ___	12. No. ___	12. No. ___	12. No. ___	12. No. ___	12. No. ___

CD Lesson #6C

Instructions: CD Lesson #6C presents two studies. Study I contrasts the No. 4 (whole–tone) with the No. 6 (chromatic) tetrachords and Study II contrasts all six basic tetrachords. Treat these drill studies as dictation exercises and fill in the blank spaces with the numbers of the corresponding and contrasting tetrachords in each column. Each ascending or descending tetrachord will be played twice with *no* sounding pitch. Listen carefully and rely on your memory before writing down your choice. Use the first (screened) answer of Study I as the model for the entire page. Answers to both studies are provided in the next chapter on page 61.

CD #1 Tracks #20(2:09) #21(2:04) #22(2:04)			CD #1 Tracks #23(2:02) #24(2:14) #25(2:07)		
Study I Contrasting No. 4 and No. 6			Study II Contrasting All Six Basic Tetrachords		
Column A	Column B	Column C	Column A	Column B	Column C
1. No. 4	1. No. ___	1. No. ___	1. No. ___	1. No. ___	1. No. ___
2. No. ___	2. No. ___	2. No. ___	2. No. ___	2. No. ___	2. No. ___
3. No. ___	3. No. ___	3. No. ___	3. No. ___	3. No. ___	3. No. ___
4. No. ___	4. No. ___	4. No. ___	4. No. ___	4. No. ___	4. No. ___
5. No. ___	5. No. ___	5. No. ___	5. No. ___	5. No. ___	5. No. ___
6. No. ___	6. No. ___	6. No. ___	6. No. ___	6. No. ___	6. No. ___
7. No. ___	7. No. ___	7. No. ___	7. No. ___	7. No. ___	7. No. ___
8. No. ___	8. No. ___	8. No. ___	8. No. ___	8. No. ___	8. No. ___
9. No. ___	9. No. ___	9. No. ___	9. No. ___	9. No. ___	9. No. ___
10. No. ___	10. No. ___	10. No. ___	10. No. ___	10. No. ___	10. No. ___
11. No. ___	11. No. ___	11. No. ___	11. No. ___	11. No. ___	11. No. ___
12. No. ___	12. No. ___	12. No. ___	12. No. ___	12. No. ___	12. No. ___

Singing Drill #7

Instructions: Singing Drill #7 presents two studies involving the combining of tetrachords to form the three forms of the minor. Study I presents the written pitches for each scale with designated tetrachords. Begin this study with the sounding of the scale's *keynote* from the piano and then go on to sing the two successive tetrachords to form the designated scale. Listen carefully and thoughtfully as you *make* each pitch. Study II presents blank staves with the designated scale and asks you to supply the key signature, pitches and hookup. After you have completed the notating of each designated scale, attempt to sing them. If you have problems with range, adjust them so that they are comfortable for singing. Start slowly and increase your speed as you become more familiar with the materials. The answers to Study II are found in the next chapter on page 62.

Study I	Study II

1. D Minor (Aeolian Form)

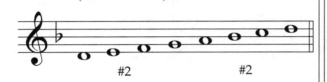

2. C Minor (Harmonic Form)

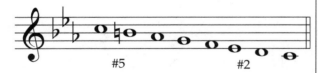

3. B♭ Minor (Melodic Form Ascending)

4. C♯ Minor (Harmonic Form)

5. B♭ Minor (Aeolian Form)

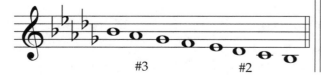

1. E Minor Melodic (Ascending)

2. G Minor (Harmonic Form, Descending)

3. F♯ Minor (Melodic Form, Descending)

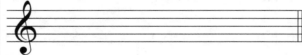

4. E♭ Minor (Harmonic Form, Ascending)

5. A Minor (Aeolian Form, Descending)

CD Lesson #7

CD #2 Tracks #1 (1:48) & #2 (2:48)

Instructions: CD Lesson #7 presents two studies involving major and minor (three forms) scales. Treat these studies as dictation exercises. In Study I name and notate each scale. Each scale will be played twice *with* a short pause between tetrachords. The interrupted bar line, placed within each blank stave, represents the dividing line between tetrachords. Study II contains twenty opportunities for identifying the scales presented. Name each one. Each scale will be played in a continuous fashion—*without* a short pause between tetrachords—and *only* once. In both studies, *middle c* or *its upper octave* will serve as the starting note for each scale. Answers to both studies are provided in the next chapter on page 63.

Study I

1. Name:_____

2. Name:_____

3. Name:_____

4. Name:_____

5. Name:_____

Study II

1. Name:_____
2. Name:_____
3. Name:_____
4. Name:_____
5. Name:_____
6. Name:_____
7. Name:_____
8. Name:_____
9. Name:_____
10. Name:_____
11. Name:_____
12. Name:_____
13. Name:_____
14. Name:_____
15. Name:_____
16. Name:_____
17. Name:_____
18. Name:_____
19. Name:_____
20. Name:_____

Singing Drill #8

Instructions: Singing Drill #8 contrasts four modes in two separate studies involving three tetrachords: No. 1 (major); No. 2 (minor); and No. 3 (Phrygian). Study I presents tetrachord segments as they would appear in a scale. Perform this study several times with the intention of memorizing it. When performing from memory, attempt to visualize, in your mind's eye, the structures of these tetrachords on a staff or keyboard or your particular instrument. This visualization process is an excellent method for quickening the pace of learning. Study II presents each of the four modes in a series of contrasting configurations. Perform these modes carefully while comparing the differences. As in previous singing drills, the adding of rhythmic interest can be extremely beneficial and productive.

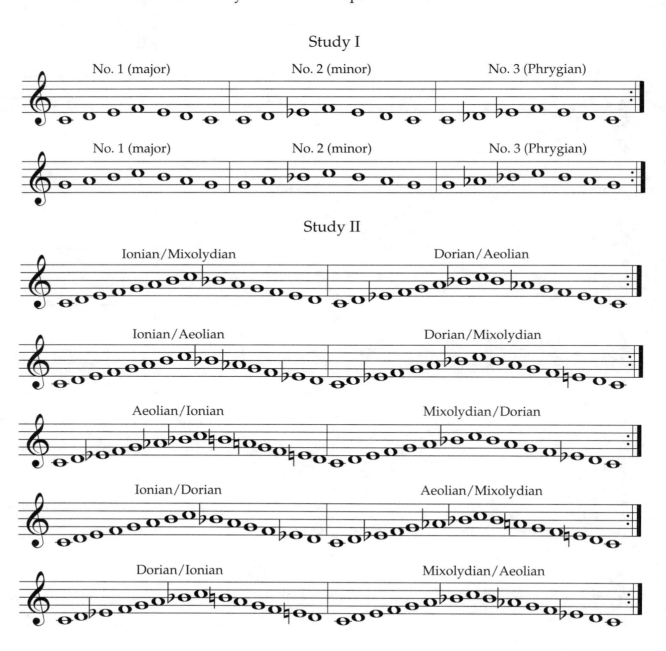

CD Lesson #8

CD #2 Tracks #3 (2:06) & #4 (3:18)

Instructions: CD Lesson #8 presents two studies involving four modes: the Ionian, Dorian, Mixolydian, and the Aeolian. Treat these studies as dictation exercises. Study I tests your ability to notate the mode with its specific tetrachords and to identify the mode by name. Each mode will be played twice *with* a short pause between tetrachords. Study II contains twenty opportunities for identifying the four modes presented. Name each one. Each mode will be played in a continuous fashion—*without* a short pause between tetrachords—and *only* once. In both studies, *middle c* or its *upper octave* will serve as the starting note for each mode. Answers to both studies are provided in the next chapter on page 64.

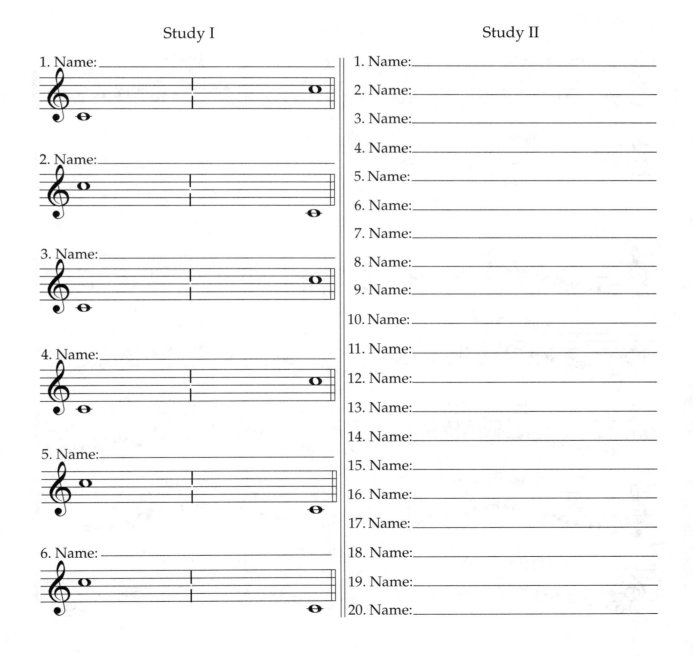

Singing Drill #9

Instructions: Singing Drill #9 contrasts four modes in two separate studies involving three tetrachords: No. 1 (major); No. 3 (Phrygian); and No. 4 (Whole-tone). Study I presents tetrachord segments as they would appear in a scale. Repeat this study several times with the intention of memorizing it. As in the previous singing drill, use the aforementioned "visualization process" to strengthen and enhance your understanding of the tetrachords. Study II presents each of the four modes in a series of contrasting configurations. Again, perform these modes carefully while comparing the differences. As in previous singing drills, the adding of rhythmic interest can be extremely beneficial and productive.

Study I

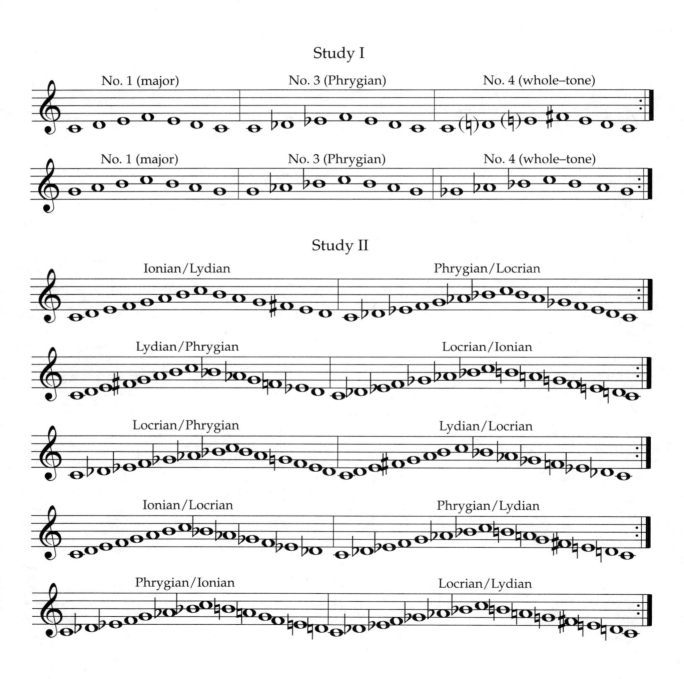

Study II

CD Lesson #9

Instructions: CD Lesson #9 presents two studies involving four modes: the Ionian, Phrygian, Lydian, and the Locrian. Treat these studies as dictation exercises. Study I tests your ability to notate the mode with its specific tetrachords and to identify the mode by name. Each ascending or descending mode is played twice *with* a short pause between tetrachords. Study II contains twenty opportunities for identifying the four modes presented. Name each one. Each ascending or descending mode is played in a continuous fashion—*without* a short pause between tetrachords—and *only* once. In both studies, *middle c* or its *upper octave* will serve as the starting note for each mode. Answers to both studies are provided in the next chapter on page 65.

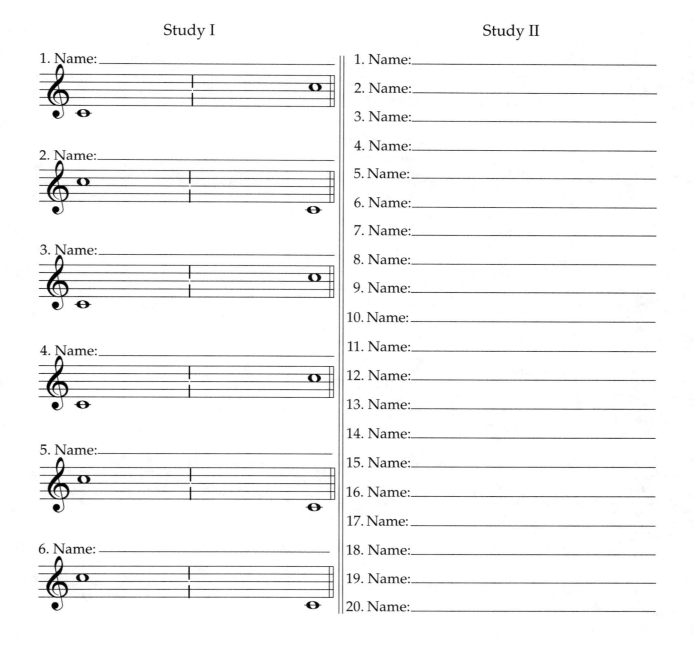

Study I

1. Name:
2. Name:
3. Name:
4. Name:
5. Name:
6. Name:

Study II

1. Name:
2. Name:
3. Name:
4. Name:
5. Name:
6. Name:
7. Name:
8. Name:
9. Name:
10. Name:
11. Name:
12. Name:
13. Name:
14. Name:
15. Name:
16. Name:
17. Name:
18. Name:
19. Name:
20. Name:

Singing Drill #10

Instructions: Singing Drill #10 contrasts pentatonic major and minor scales along with whole–tone scales in two studies involving three tetrachords: No. 1 (major), No. 2 (minor), and No. 4 (whole–tone). Study I presents tetrachord segments (both abbreviated and regular) as they appear in scale form. Study II presents pentatonic and whole–tone scales in a series of contrasting configurations. As an added feature of this study, the chromatic scale is included as well. Perform all of these scales carefully while comparing the differences. As in previous singing drills, the adding of rhythmic interest can be extremely beneficial and productive.

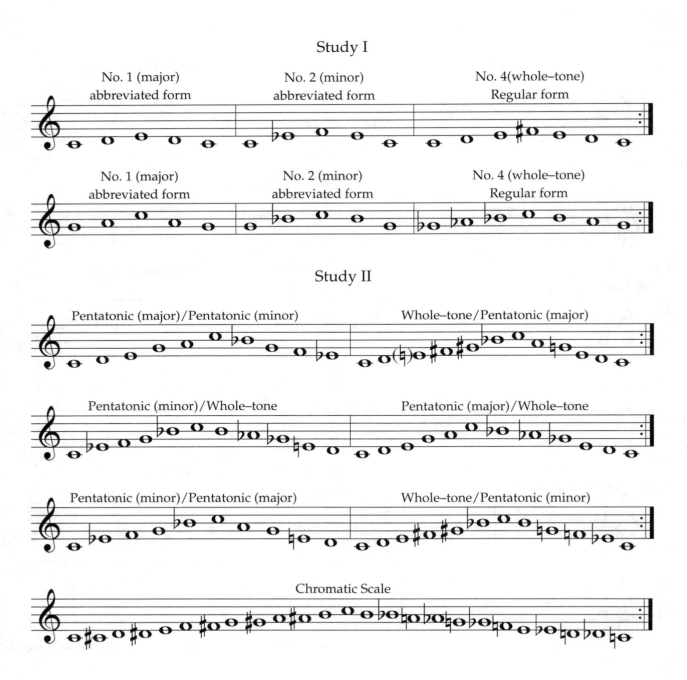

CD Lesson #10A

CD #2 Tracks #7 (3:12) & #8 (5:15)

Instructions: CD Lesson #10A presents two studies involving pentatonic, whole–tone, and chromatic scales. Treat these studies as dictation exercises. Study I tests your ability to name and notate scales. Because of the use of abbreviated tetrachords, pentatonic, whole-tone, and chromatic scales will contain short, appropriately placed pauses within each scale type. Each scale will be played twice. Study II affords you twenty opportunities to identify each type of scale. Name each one. These ascending or descending scales will be played in a continuous fashion—*without* short pauses—and *only* once. In both studies, *middle c* or its *upper octave* will serve as the starting note for each scale. Answers to both studies are provided in the next chapter on page 66.

Study I

1. Name:_____

2. Name:_____

3. Name:_____

4. Name:_____

5. Name:_____

6. Name:_____

Study II

1. Name:_____
2. Name:_____
3. Name:_____
4. Name:_____
5. Name:_____
6. Name:_____
7. Name:_____
8. Name:_____
9. Name:_____
10. Name:_____
11. Name:_____
12. Name:_____
13. Name:_____
14. Name:_____
15. Name:_____
16. Name:_____
17. Name:_____
18. Name:_____
19. Name:_____
20. Name:_____

CD Lesson #10B

CD #2 Tracks #9 (5:55) & #10 (5:30)

Instructions: CD Lesson #10B presents two studies involving all the tetrachords and scales presented. Treat these studies as dictation exercises and name each one. Each study contains twenty–five opportunities to identify ascending or descending scales and chromatic fragments. These scales and fragments are played in a continuous fashion—without pauses—and *only* once. Feel free to use the pause button on your CD if you are having difficulty; however, every effort should be made to work within the time limits of the CD. In both studies, a variety of starting notes are used. Use the first (screened) answer of Study I as the model for the entire page. Answers to both studies are provided in the next chapter on page 67.

Study I

1. Name: Minor or Aeolian Mode - Asc.
2. Name:
3. Name:
4. Name:
5. Name:
6. Name:
7. Name:
8. Name:
9. Name:
10. Name:
11. Name:
12. Name:
13. Name:
14. Name:
15. Name:
16. Name:
17. Name:
18. Name:
19. Name:
20. Name:
21. Name:
22. Name:
23. Name:
24. Name:
25. Name:

Study II

1. Name:
2. Name:
3. Name:
4. Name:
5. Name:
6. Name:
7. Name:
8. Name:
9. Name:
10. Name:
11. Name:
12. Name:
13. Name:
14. Name:
15. Name:
16. Name:
17. Name:
18. Name:
19. Name:
20. Name:
21. Name:
22. Name:
23. Name:
24. Name:
25. Name:

CD Lesson #10C

CD #2 Tracks #11 (5:52) & #12 (5:48)

Instructions: CD Lesson #10C presents an additional opportunity to identify tetrachords, scales, and chromatic fragments. Again, treat these studies as dictation exercises and name each one. Apply the same instructions to this page as were given for the previous page. After you have named each exercise and completed these studies as directed, do them orally; in addition, start and stop the CD at various places to help defeat any unintended memorization that might take place involving a particular scale order. Both procedures will help keep these studies fresh and more interesting. Attempt to stay within the allotted time for each exercise. Answers to both studies are given in the next chapter on page 68.

Study I

1. Name: harmonic minor (ascending)
2. Name: _____
3. Name: _____
4. Name: _____
5. Name: _____
6. Name: _____
7. Name: _____
8. Name: _____
9. Name: _____
10. Name: _____
11. Name: _____
12. Name: _____
13. Name: _____
14. Name: _____
15. Name: _____
16. Name: _____
17. Name: _____
18. Name: _____
19. Name: _____
20. Name: _____
21. Name: _____
22. Name: _____
23. Name: _____
24. Name: _____
25. Name: _____

Study II

1. Name: _____
2. Name: _____
3. Name: _____
4. Name: _____
5. Name: _____
6. Name: _____
7. Name: _____
8. Name: _____
9. Name: _____
10. Name: _____
11. Name: _____
12. Name: _____
13. Name: _____
14. Name: _____
15. Name: _____
16. Name: _____
17. Name: _____
18. Name: _____
19. Name: _____
20. Name: _____
21. Name: _____
22. Name: _____
23. Name: _____
24. Name: _____
25. Name: _____

MANUSCRIPT PRACTICE
Use empty staves for note taking and drill.

SCALE FORMS

through

SIX BASIC TETRACHORDS

CHAPTER **IV**

CD Answers

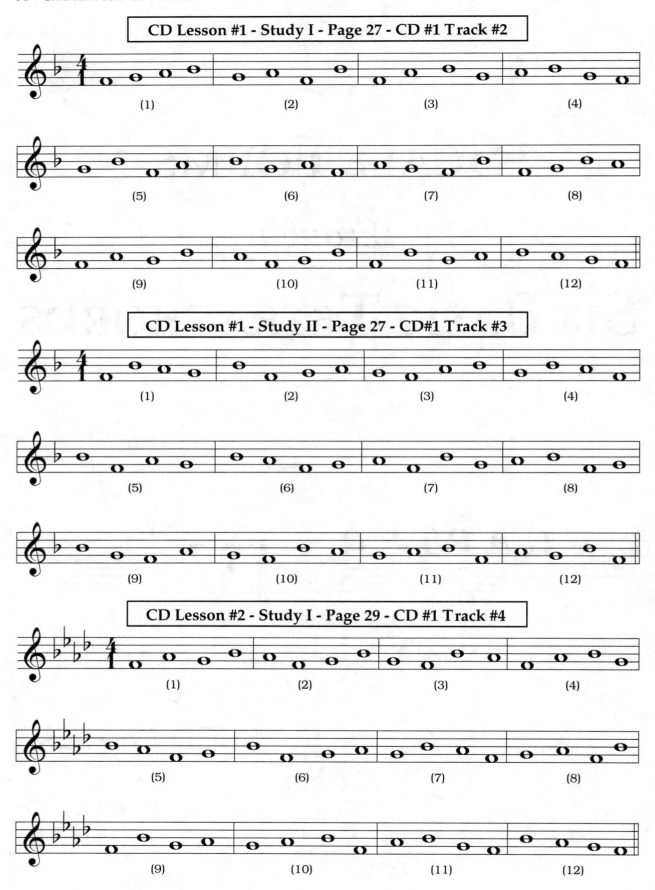

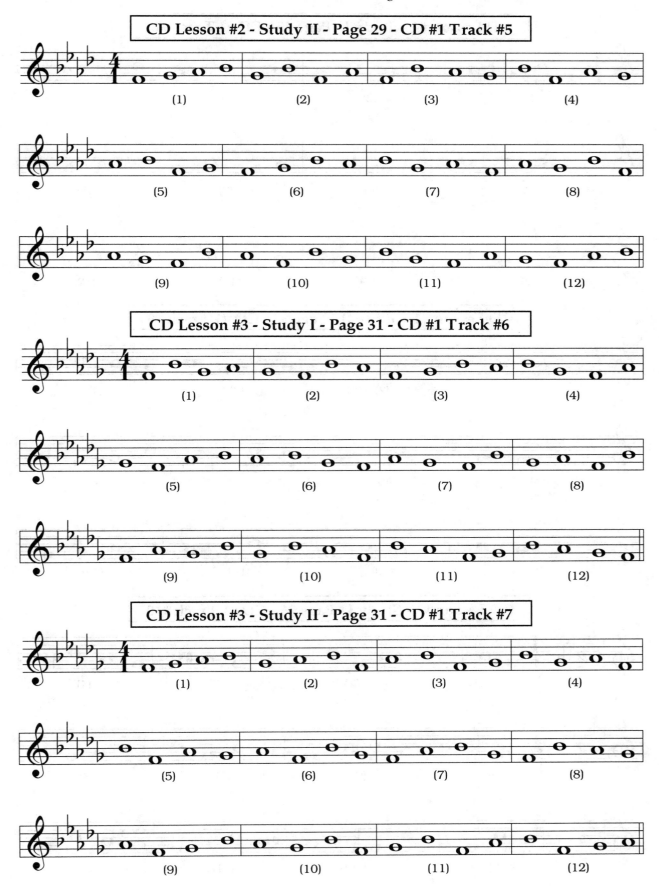

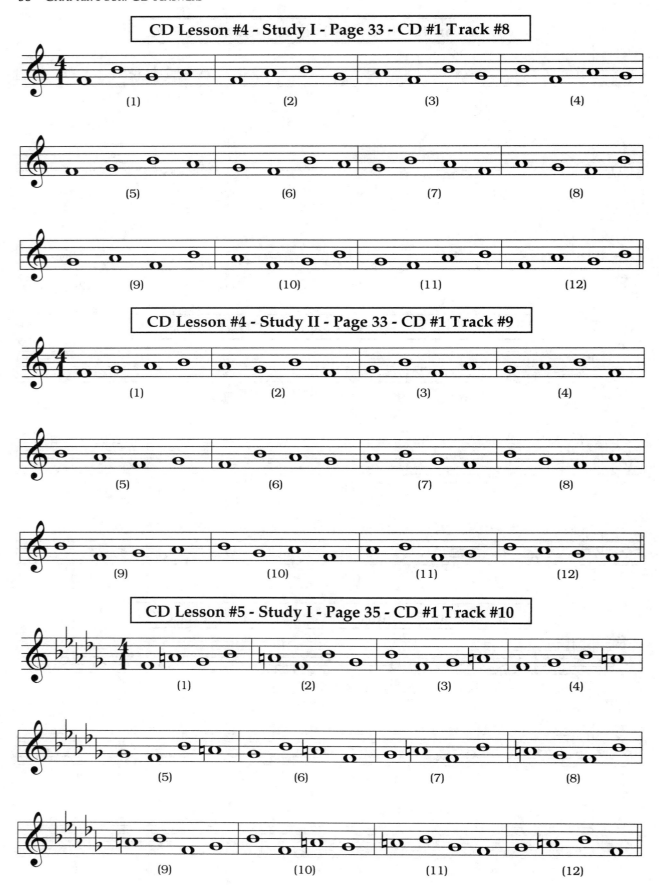

CD Lesson #4 - Study I - Page 33 - CD #1 Track #8

(1)   (2)   (3)   (4)

(5)   (6)   (7)   (8)

(9)   (10)   (11)   (12)

CD Lesson #4 - Study II - Page 33 - CD #1 Track #9

(1)   (2)   (3)   (4)

(5)   (6)   (7)   (8)

(9)   (10)   (11)   (12)

CD Lesson #5 - Study I - Page 35 - CD #1 Track #10

(1)   (2)   (3)   (4)

(5)   (6)   (7)   (8)

(9)   (10)   (11)   (12)

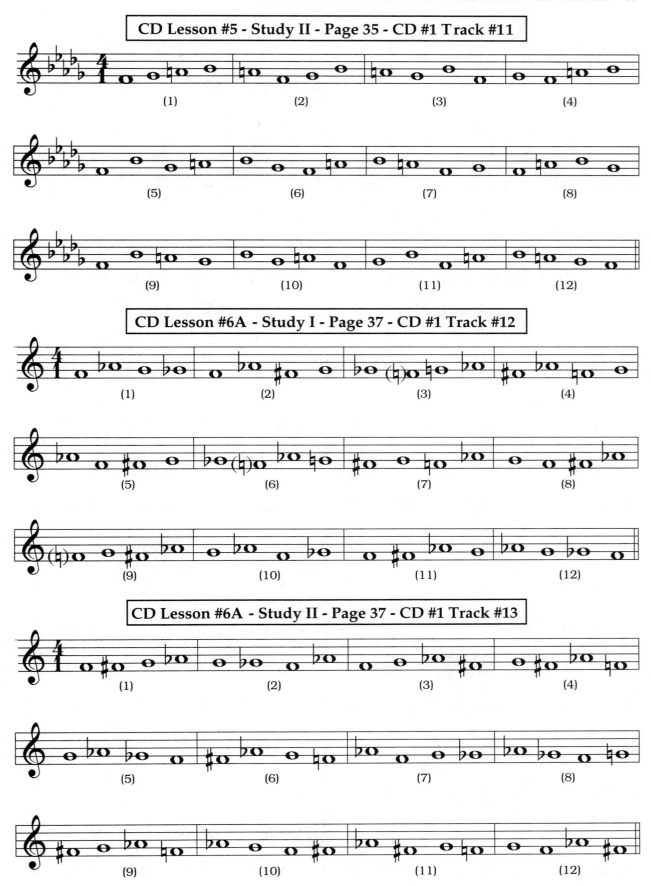

CD Lesson #6B - Study I - Page 38	CD Lesson #6B - Study II - Page 38

CD #1 Track #14, #15 & #16	**CD #1 Track #17, 18, & #19**
Contrasting No. 1 and No. 2	Contrasting No. 3 and No. 5

Column A	Column B	Column C	Column A	Column B	Column C
1. No. 1	1. No. 2	1. No. 2	1. No. 3	1. No. 5	1. No. 3
2. No. 2	2. No. 1	2. No. 2	2. No. 5	2. No. 3	2. No. 5
3. No. 2	3. No. 2	3. No. 1	3. No. 5	3. No. 3	3. No. 3
4. No. 1	4. No. 2	4. No. 1	4. No. 3	4. No. 5	4. No. 5
5. No. 2	5. No. 1	5. No. 2	5. No. 3	5. No. 5	5. No. 3
6. No. 2	6. No. 2	6. No. 1	6. No. 5	6. No. 3	6. No. 5
7. No. 1	7. No. 1	7. No. 2	7. No. 3	7. No. 5	7. No. 5
8. No. 1	8. No. 2	8. No. 2	8. No. 5	8. No. 3	8. No. 3
9. No. 2	9. No. 1	9. No. 1	9. No. 3	9. No. 5	9. No. 3
10. No. 1	10. No. 2	10. No. 1	10. No. 5	10. No. 3	10. No. 5
11. No. 1	11. No. 1	11. No. 2	11. No. 3	11. No. 5	11. No. 3
12. No. 2	12. No. 1	12. No. 1	12. No. 5	12. No. 3	12. No. 5

CD Lesson #6C - Study I - Page 39	CD Lesson #6C - Study II - Page 39

CD #1 Track #20, #21, & #22 **CD #1 Track #23, #24, & #25**

Contrasting No. 4 and No. 6

Contrasting All Six Basic Tetrachords

Column A	Column B	Column C	Column A	Column B	Column C
1. No. 4	1. No. 4	1. No. 4	1. No. 1	1. No. 6	1. No. 3
2. No. 6	2. No. 4	2. No. 6	2. No. 6	2. No. 3	2. No. 5
3. No. 4	3. No. 6	3. No. 6	3. No. 5	3. No. 4	3. No. 2
4. No. 6	4. No. 4	4. No. 4	4. No. 1	4. No. 2	4. No. 6
5. No. 6	5. No. 6	5. No. 4	5. No. 4	5. No. 6	5. No. 1
6. No. 4	6. No. 4	6. No. 6	6. No. 3	6. No. 5	6. No. 4
7. No. 4	7. No. 6	7. No. 4	7. No. 6	7. No. 3	7. No. 5
8. No. 6	8. No. 6	8. No. 6	8. No. 2	8. No. 1	8. No. 6
9. No. 4	9. No. 6	9. No. 4	9. No. 4	9. No. 4	9. No. 4
10. No. 4	10. No. 4	10. No. 6	10. No. 3	10. No. 5	10. No. 1
11. No. 6	11. No. 6	11. No. 4	11. No. 2	11. No. 2	11. No. 2
12. No. 6	12. No. 4	12. No. 6	12. No. 5	12. No. 1	12. No. 3

Singing Drill #7 - Study II - Page 40

Study II

1. E Minor Melodic (Ascending)

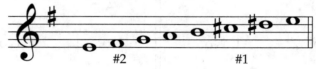

2. G Minor (Harmonic Form, Descending)

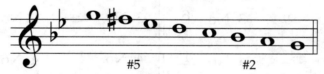

3. F♯ Minor (Melodic Form, Descending)

4. E♭ Minor (Harmonic Form, Ascending)

5. A Minor (Aeolian Form, Descending)

| CD Lesson #7 - Study I - Page 41 | CD Lesson #7 - Study II - Page 41 |

CD #2 Track #1

CD #2 Track #2

1. Name: C Major Scale

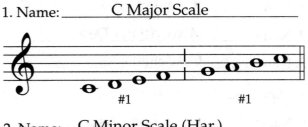

#1   #1

2. Name: C Minor Scale (Har.)

#5   #2

3. Name: C Minor Scale (Mel.)

#2   #1

4. Name: C Minor Scale (Aeol.)

#2   #3

5. Name: C Major Scale

#1   #1

1. Name: C Major Scale - Asc.
2. Name: C Minor Scale (Aeol.) - Asc.
3. Name: C Minor Scale (Har.) - Asc.
4. Name: C Major Scale - Desc.
5. Name: C Minor Scale (Aeol.) - Desc.
6. Name: C Minor Scale (Har.) - Desc.
7. Name: C Minor Scale (Mel.) - Asc.
8. Name: C Major Scale - Desc.
9. Name: C Minor Scale (Har.) - Asc.
10. Name: C Major Scale - Asc.
11. Name: C Minor Scale (Har.) - Asc.
12. Name: C Major Scale - Desc.
13. Name: C Minor Scale (Aeol.) - Asc.
14. Name: C Minor Scale (Mel.) - Asc.
15. Name: C Minor Scale (Har.) - Desc.
16. Name: C Minor Scale (Mel.) - Asc.
17. Name: C Minor Scale (Aeol.) - Desc.
18. Name: C Major Scale - Asc.
19. Name: C Minor Scale (Har.) - Desc.
20. Name: C Minor Scale (Mel.) - Asc.

| CD Lesson #8 - Study I - Page 43 | CD Lesson #8 - Study II - Page 43 |

CD #2 Track #3

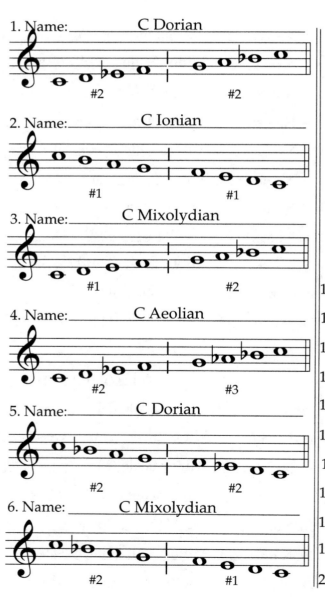

1. Name: _____ C Dorian _____
2. Name: _____ C Ionian _____
3. Name: _____ C Mixolydian _____
4. Name: _____ C Aeolian _____
5. Name: _____ C Dorian _____
6. Name: _____ C Mixolydian _____

CD #2 Track #4

1. Name: _____ C Ionian - Asc. _____
2. Name: _____ C Mixolydian - Desc. _____
3. Name: _____ C Aoelian - Asc. _____
4. Name: _____ C Mixolydian - Asc. _____
5. Name: _____ C Aoelian - Asc. _____
6. Name: _____ C Mixolydian - Desc. _____
7. Name: _____ C Dorian - Asc. _____
8. Name: _____ C Mixolydian - Asc. _____
9. Name: _____ C Dorian - Asc. _____
10. Name: _____ C Ionian - Desc. _____
11. Name: _____ C Dorian - Asc. _____
12. Name: _____ C Mixolydian - Desc. _____
13. Name: _____ C Aeolian - Desc. _____
14. Name: _____ C Dorian - Desc. _____
15. Name: _____ C Mixolydian - Asc. _____
16. Name: _____ C Dorian - Desc. _____
17. Name: _____ C Mixolydian - Asc. _____
18. Name: _____ C Aeolian - Desc. _____
19. Name: _____ C Mixolydian - Desc. _____
20. Name: _____ C Dorian - Desc. _____

CD Lesson #9 - Study I - Page 45	CD Lesson #9 - Study II - Page 45

CD #2 Track #5

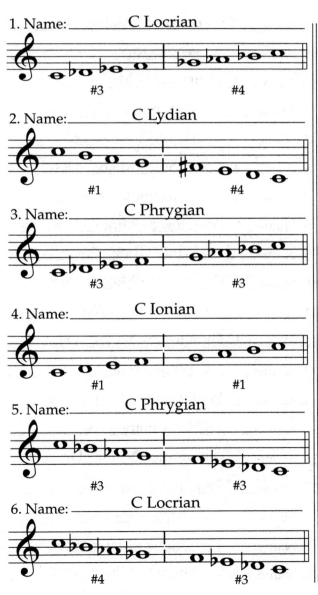

1. Name: C Locrian

    #3   #4

2. Name: C Lydian

    #1   #4

3. Name: C Phrygian

    #3   #3

4. Name: C Ionian

    #1   #1

5. Name: C Phrygian

    #3   #3

6. Name: C Locrian

    #4   #3

CD #2 Track #6

1. Name: C Ionian - Asc.
2. Name: C Phrygian - Asc.
3. Name: C Locrian - Desc.
4. Name: C Phrygian - Desc.
5. Name: C Locrian - Asc.
6. Name: C Ionian - Desc.
7. Name: C Lydian - Asc.
8. Name: C Phrygian - Asc.
9. Name: C Locrian - Desc.
10. Name: C Lydian - Desc.
11. Name: C Phrygian - Desc.
12. Name: C Ionian - Asc.
13. Name: C Phrygian - Asc.
14. Name: C Lydian - Desc.
15. Name: C Phrygian - Asc.
16. Name: C Lydian - Asc.
17. Name: C Locrian - Asc.
18. Name: C Ionian - Desc.
19. Name: C Phrygian - Desc.
20. Name: C Lydian - Asc.

CD Lesson #10A - Study I - Page 47

CD Lesson #10A - Study II - Page 47

CD #2 Track #7

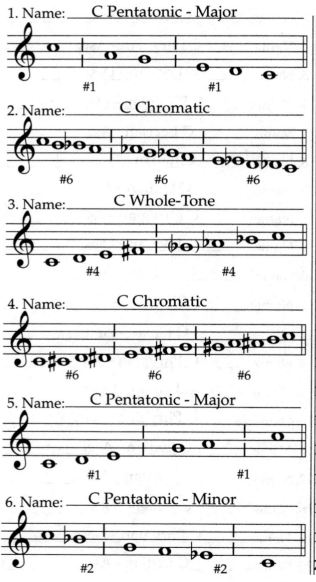

1. Name: C Pentatonic - Major
   #1   #1

2. Name: C Chromatic
   #6   #6   #6

3. Name: C Whole-Tone
   #4   #4

4. Name: C Chromatic
   #6   #6   #6

5. Name: C Pentatonic - Major
   #1   #1

6. Name: C Pentatonic - Minor
   #2   #2

CD #2 Track #8

1. Name: C Pentatonic - Major - Asc.

2. Name: C Whole-Tone - Desc.

3. Name: C Pentatonic - Minor - Asc.

4. Name: C Chromatic - Desc.

5. Name: C Whole-Tone - Asc.

6. Name: C Pentatonic - Major - Desc.

7. Name: C Chromatic - Asc.

8. Name: C Pentatonic - Minor - Desc.

9. Name: C Whole-Tone - Asc.

10. Name: C Pentatonic - Major - Desc.

11. Name: C Chromatic - Asc.

12. Name: C Pentatonic - Minor - Desc.

13. Name: C Whole-Tone-Asc.

14. Name: C Pentatonic - Major - Desc.

15. Name: C Chromatic - Asc.

16. Name: C Pentatonic - Major - Desc.

17. Name: C Pentatonic - Minor - Asc.

18. Name: C Chromatic - Desc.

19. Name: C Pentatonic - Major - Asc.

20. Name: C Pentatonic - Minor - Desc.

| CD Lesson #10B - Study I - Page 48 | CD Lesson #10B - Study II - Page 48 |

CD #2 Track #9

1. Name: Minor or Aeolian Mode - Asc.
2. Name: Pentatonic - Major - Asc.
3. Name: Dorian Mode - Desc.
4. Name: Lydian Mode - Asc.
5. Name: Major or Ionian Mode - Desc.
6. Name: Minor - Har. - Asc.
7. Name: Pentatonic - Major - Asc.
8. Name: Lydian Mode - Desc.
9. Name: Chromatic - Desc.
10. Name: Minor - Har. - Desc.
11. Name: Phrygian - Mode - Asc.
12. Name: Whole-Tone - Desc.
13. Name: Minor or Aeolian Mode - Asc.
14. Name: Whole-Tone - Asc.
15. Name: Mixolydian Mode - Desc.
16. Name: Major or Ionian Mode - Asc.
17. Name: Locrian - Desc.
18. Name: Pentatonic - Minor - Asc.
19. Name: Minor or Aeolian Mode - Desc.
20. Name: Chromatic - Asc.
21. Name: Dorian Mode - Asc.
22. Name: Pentatonic - Minor - Desc.
23. Name: Mixolydian Mode - Asc.
24. Name: Locrian Mode - Asc.
25. Name: Minor or Aeolian Mode - Asc.

CD #2 Track #10

1. Name: Minor - Har. - Asc.
2. Name: Lydian Mode - Asc.
3. Name: Phrygian Mode - Desc.
4. Name: Whole-Tone - Desc.
5. Name: Pentatonic - Minor - Asc.
6. Name: Minor - Mel. - Asc.
7. Name: Major or Ionian - Asc.
8. Name: Dorian Mode - Asc.
9. Name: Pentatonic - Major - Asc.
10. Name: Locrian Mode - Desc.
11. Name: Dorian Mode - Asc.
12. Name: Chromatic - Asc.
13. Name: Pentatonic - Minor - Desc.
14. Name: Mixolydion Mode - Desc.
15. Name: Dorian Mode - Asc.
16. Name: Locrian Mode - Asc.
17. Name: Mixolydian Mode - Asc.
18. Name: Phrygian Mode - Asc.
19. Name: Pentatonic - Major - Desc.
20. Name: Major or Ionian Mode - Desc.
21. Name: Lydian Mode - Desc.
22. Name: Whole-Tone - Asc.
23. Name: Minor - Har. - Desc.
24. Name: Chromatic - Desc.
25. Name: Minor or Aeolian Mode - Desc.

CD Lesson #10C - Study I - Page 49	CD Lesson #10C - Study II - Page 49

CD #2 Track #11

1. Name: Minor Har. - Asc.
2. Name: Pentatonic - Minor - Desc.
3. Name: Minor Mel. - Asc.
4. Name: Locrian Mode - Asc.
5. Name: Minor or Aeolian Mode - Asc.
6. Name: Pentatonic - Major - Asc.
7. Name: Major or Ionian Mode - Asc.
8. Name: Dorian Mode - Desc.
9. Name: Phrygian Mode - Asc.
10. Name: Mixolydian Mode - Desc.
11. Name: Dorian Mode - Asc.
12. Name: Whole-Tone - Desc.
13. Name: Lydian Mode - Asc.
14. Name: Pentatonic Minor - Asc.
15. Name: Lydian Mode - Desc.
16. Name: Locrian Mode - Asc.
17. Name: Major or Ionian Mode - Asc.
18. Name: Mixolydian Mode - Asc.
19. Name: Phrygian Mode - Desc.
20. Name: Minor or Aeolian Mode - Asc.
21. Name: Minor Har. - Desc.
22. Name: Chromatic - Asc.
23. Name: Pentatonic Minor - Desc.
24. Name: Chromatic - Desc.
25. Name: Whole-Tone - Asc.

CD #2 Track #12

1. Name: Pentatonic - Major - Asc.
2. Name: Dorian Mode - Desc.
3. Name: Minor Har. - Asc.
4. Name: Phrygian Mode - Desc.
5. Name: Pentatonic Major - Desc.
6. Name: Locrian Mode - Asc.
7. Name: Pentatonic Minor - Desc.
8. Name: Major or Ionian Mode - Asc.
9. Name: Major or Ionian Mode Desc.
10. Name: Mixolydian Mode - Desc.
11. Name: Minor Mel. - Asc.
12. Name: Minor Har. - Desc.
13. Name: Whole-Tone - Asc.
14. Name: Lydian Mode - Desc.
15. Name: Minor or Aeolian Mode - Asc.
16. Name: Chromatic - Desc.
17. Name: Pentatonic Minor - Asc.
18. Name: Whole-Tone - Desc.
19. Name: Mixolydian - Asc.
20. Name: Locrian Mode - Desc.
21. Name: Major or Ionian - Asc.
22. Name: Minor or Aeolian Mode - Desc.
23. Name: Chromatic - Asc.
24. Name: Dorian Mode - Asc.
25. Name: Pentatonic Major - Asc.

EAR TRAINING

VOLUME I

SCALE FORMS *THROUGH* SIX BASIC TETRACHORDS

ISBN: 0-9620941-2-9 © 2002

CD #1

CD #2

Index